I0441872

RACE AGAINST
MOTHER NATURE

Lorna Daniel

authorHOUSE®

AuthorHouse™
1663 Liberty Drive
Bloomington, IN 47403
www.authorhouse.com
Phone: 1 (800) 839-8640

© 2018 Lorna Daniel. All rights reserved.

No part of this book may be reproduced, stored in a retrieval system, or transmitted by any means without the written permission of the author.

Published by AuthorHouse 01/17/2020

ISBN: 978-1-5462-6243-5 (sc)
ISBN: 978-1-5462-6242-8 (e)

Print information available on the last page.

This book is printed on acid-free paper.

Because of the dynamic nature of the Internet, any web addresses or links contained in this book may have changed since publication and may no longer be valid. The views expressed in this work are solely those of the author and do not necessarily reflect the views of the publisher, and the publisher hereby disclaims any responsibility for them.

ACKNOWLEDGEMENTS

To my C.A.H.S family, especially Aimee, April, Chervell, Iambakisye, Joel, Melony, Sharon, thanks for your unwavering support. To my longtime friend Wendy Francis, thanks for your continued guidance and advice thus far. To my family and friends thank you for the moral support, especially Jhozna and Jovonn, you are my inspiration.

CHAPTER 1

Summer Heat

How unbearably hot and humid were the long days and nights of the summer of 2017! Residents of the small, beautiful Virgin Islands, which are uniquely located in the historic Caribbean and bordered by both the Caribbean Sea and the Atlantic Ocean, were tired of the heat and prayed earnestly for rain. The battle with the heat drove many residents to the crowded white sand beaches; some even visited twice, or three times, a day. The days passed by with little or no breeze blowing, and many residents could be seen on their verandah drinking lemonade or a local favorite - passion fruit juice. This was an escape from the furnace-like, stifling outdoors and a break from the baking heat indoors. The broiling heat was also an opportunity to indulge in eating the ripe, juicy mangoes which are usually in great abundance during the summer. Summer 2017 had mangoes everywhere! Mangoes were seen falling from trees and carpeting the entire spread of neighbors' yards. One old lady wisely remarked, "This is too much mangoes for one mango season. Something brewing. A big hurricane coming. Ah feel it in meh old bones." Only a few older residents believed in her predictions, the young ones mocked and remarked laughingly, "Old people always have a story to tell."

Erma Matthew, a thirteen year old, longed for the summer's heat wave to pass. She was one of the many residents who sought relief in the cooling waters of the many beaches that surround the island of St. Thomas. When she was not at the beach, she would visit neighboring relatives or download and play games on her phone and iPad since she was technologically savvy. She was also an avid reader and read many books from her iPad. In fact, for her, there was no limit to the uses of her iPad. Being a typical modern-day teenager, social media was, of course, a big part of her daily activities; she talked, texted, and tweeted over and over when she wasn't watching the latest "Snaps."

"I am bored, Mom!" Erma yelled to her mother, Marjorie, one day. "I am ready for school to start."

Erma's mother rolled her eyes and remarked under her breath, "I'm bored! I'm bored!: The motto of the young." Out loud, she responded, "Go read a book."

Erma was longing to be reacquainted with her friends and to share her experiences during the long summer vacation about her trip to the other Caribbean islands. Last school year, Erma was on the Honor Roll and was one of the highest performing students in her class. As a reward for her diligence in her school work, her family took her on a Caribbean cruise. Erma and her family visited the historical islands of St. Kitts and Nevis, Antigua, St. Lucia, and Curacao. Erma was in awe when she saw those islands for the first time; she was fascinated with their individual beauty. Each island had something exclusively different that set it apart from the others, but one thing rang common among them - that feeling of being home. Each island had, on full display, the warm, kind, and friendly nature of the Caribbean people. This year, however, the heat seemed to follow Erma on each leg of her trip. She eventually purchased a pair of sun glasses and a wide-brimmed hat to protect her beautiful eyes and skin. To show all her friends that she was not just "stunting for the Gram" and to show that her voyage did indeed happen, Erma purchased a few souvenirs to take back to school and to give to her favorite friends Jhazarra, K'shawn, Kezia, Shaddai, and Zaria.

With August almost over, Erma perked up as she heard the local radio station announce that the new academic school year was slated to begin on the Tuesday after Labor Day. She even heard that some schools had orientations scheduled for the week before Labor Day. Erma was thrilled! The long, hot, slow, and boring days were almost over. Immediately, her demeanor changed; her shoulders lifted, and she patted the strands of her short, black, natural hair with pride. Her long brown fingers hid a smile that tugged at the corners of her lips, and her dark brown eyes glowed with excitement as she recalled her fun filled summer vacation. "At last!" she thought to herself, "I'll finally get to see my friends and share my exciting encounters." It is not that she could not call her friends and speak to them, or even video chat or Facetime them, but they made an agreement to save their summer stories for when they returned to school, and the wait was killing Erma. There was no doubt that it was killing her friends too. Her school bag was already packed with her books and the few souvenirs she brought back for her friends from around the Caribbean. Erma resolved that she would do even better in her course work this school year. In fact, over her summer break, she created a theme for the new school year: "Overcoming roadblocks with discipline and determination."

CHAPTER 2

Pressure Drop

Marjorie, Erma's mother, as usual, listened to the local news every morning at 6:30 a.m.; but that morning, she kept listening to the radio and muttering under her breath, "I can't believe what I am hearing." The radio crackled and sputtered as Marjorie tried to tune in to the news. Since the static seemed to be getting worse, and Erma Marjorie had difficulty understanding what the radio announcer was saying, Erma decided to walk down to the nearby convenience shop and purchased a copy of the local newspaper *The Daily News*. Marjorie was on the verandah waiting when Erma returned. Something peculiar was happening. Erma could feel the tension in the air. She looked towards Erma as she climbed the steps with the paper rolled up in her hand. As if in response to a silent question, Erma shook her head rapidly, waving the paper in the air. Inside, Marjorie sat on the sofa and opened up the newspaper. Then came a sound, like a moan, "Oh No! No! No!" As she read the headline, Marjorie laid back on her sofa and held her head between her hands and groaned.

"What's happening?" Erma asked, but she received no response from her mom. Finally, after what seemed like an eternity, Marjorie put the newspaper down and left the room. Erma quickly moved over and grabbed the paper. As she read, she discovered that a hurricane was approaching the northern Leeward Islands and apparently the Virgin Islands was in its mapped path.

Geography was once Erma's favorite subject; she already knew how to locate many of the various islands on a map. She could identify the Virgin Islands and British Virgin Islands, the Windward Islands, Leeward Islands, Greater Antilles, Lesser Antilles, and the ABC Islands which were located to the west of Trinidad and Tobago. She quickly took out the hurricane tracking map that her Geography teacher distributed in class last year. She skillfully shaded the northern Leeward Islands. Erma then plotted the coordinates and realized that, at present, the storm was at 17° North and 50° West. Is this why her mother is so upset? She thinks the Virgin Islands are going to get hit. Well, as Erma remembered, the Virgin Islands were 18° North and 64° West. If the storm travelled northwest, it might not happen. Erma felt that she had ample time to prepare for the storm, so she continued to watch her favorite television program, unperturbed by the news of the approaching storm, and unaware that this hurricane was moving southwest and forecasted to turn to the northwest over the course of the Labor Day weekend.

According to Marjorie, the radio announcer kept saying that the storm was definitely heading their way, and they needed to make sure they had water, batteries, and all sorts of non-perishable items in preparation for the approaching storm. Neighbors kept calling out to Marjorie as they passed by, asking her if she heard about the hurricane and if she was not going to the supermarket to get extra stuff. Finally, Marjorie agreed that she should go shopping after all. She said wearily, "Come. Let's follow the crowd and get some non-perishable items and batteries in preparation for this storm." Her weariness gave way to disgust as she followed up angrily with, "She needs to know her place and stay out of our beautiful and pristine Caribbean Islands." She took an unconcerned Erma along with her. Instead of going to the neighborhood shop, which was already without bottled water, they went to the closest large supermarket to shop. They drove to three other supermarkets, but there were no parking spaces available. Finally, they stopped at the one nearest to their home.

When they finally got inside, it was a surprise to witness how the aisles were packed with people rushing about and grabbing all sorts of things from the shelves. People with anxious, worried faces seemed to be in a panic. Erma and her mother bought many non-perishable items such as cans of tuna, peas, and vegetables. Batteries were almost sold out, but they managed to get the last two packs and the last large flash light that was left behind. When they got to the water area, it was chaos. Marjory had to bulldoze her way between people, and she was lucky to emerge with a case of water in hand. "Erma," she said shamefully, "sorry you have to see me displaying this rude behavior, but in this situation each one to himself."

Back in the car with all the shopping bags packed in the trunk, they turned on the car radio. Erma grew alarmed as she listened to the announcer's voice coming through the speakers. "The storm that developed off the coast of Africa about a week ago has intensified. It is now a Category Three hurricane, and on its projected path, could reach the Northern Leeward Islands by the early part of the week." Erma looked at her mother. The crease in her forehead, that appeared the day she saw the newspaper, seemed to have taken permanent residence and her normal joyful countenance now appeared serious and worried at the same time. She looked tortured. Erma wished there was something she could do just to see a smile on her mother's face; but instead, she heard herself saying, "Stop worrying, Mom. Everything will be alright." Her voice was soft and calm in an attempt to soothe her mother. Erma began softly humming Bob Marley's song "Three Little Birds." When Erma reached the verse, "Don't worry. Everything's gonna be alright," she raised her voice so that her mother could hear her. Marjorie eventually produced a smile and began to sing along with her.

At the end of that encouraging song, everything was quiet in the car. No one spoke for the rest of the drive home. Erma recalled that at one of the Saturday's meetings of the Young Fire Fighters Club, a small group from the American Red Cross visited them and spoke to the club members about "The Pillow Case Project." They gave each person a pillowcase and discussed with them the items that they should take with them in case there was a natural disaster that required evacuation from their home to a shelter. Once home, Erma took out her pillowcase and stuffed it with her favorite books, her teddy bear named Chummy, and a flashlight. She remembered that her mother had another small transistor radio; so she packed it, along with some of the batteries that were bought.

Feelings of excitement and dread hung in the air at the same. Erma could not help, but she felt a bit nervous. Outside, the atmosphere had a kind of stillness and calm. Occasionally, only a gentle breeze could be felt. Everywhere she turned, whether for a walk around her neighborhood or just looking over her veranda, there was someone talking about the fast approaching hurricane with the name "Irma."

Erma cringed when she learned that the hurricane's name, "Irma," sounded just like her name. Mentally, she prepared herself for some teasing from her classmates and friends when it would be all over. She knew the heckling and teasing were coming. There was no escape here. That Sunday night, Erma overheard her elderly neighbor, and her prayer group, clapping their hands and praying and singing loudly, hoping that the hurricane would either change its direction or dissipate in the Atlantic Ocean. Silently, Erma wished the same. Even the young men were gathering and talking about the approaching hurricane while playing dominoes outside under the big mango tree. The young women were busy making a list about what to buy and changing their appointments with their hairdressers.

CHAPTER 3

Imminent Irma

The opening of the new school year was no longer the topic of conversation for members of this small Caribbean community. All eyes were now fixed on the Weather Channel and ears were glued to the local radio stations. Erma's friends kept texting her, already teasing and mocking her about the approaching hurricane. She reminded them that her name began with an "E" instead of an "I." Plus, she insisted, "This is no time to be joking. A hurricane is about to hit our island." But they paid her no mind. No one her age cared! They called her on her cell phone chanting, "Irma is coming!" "Don't let her drown ya!" To avoid the persistent heckling, Erma eventually turned off her cell phone, telling herself that she needed to save the battery, anyhow. She was annoyed and wished that they would grow up and act more responsibly.

"Hurricane Irma has now been upgraded to a Category Four storm and the Virgin Islands are definitely projected to be in its path," said the once preppy announcer in a nervous voice. The radio blasted out the undesirable news, as Erma entered the kitchen where her mother was. Like many others, Marjorie and Erma decided to go back to the store to buy some more batteries, cases of bottled water, and other groceries. The supermarket was even more crowded with people than the last time when they were there. People were now in full panic mode. "It's Marilyn all over again!" some whispered. "No, it is Hugo reincarnated," others sighed. Erma wondered what they were talking about and did not ask; but Marjorie explained in a soft voice that although she was but a mere teenager at the time of Hurricane Hugo, she could still vividly recall the pain and suffering that was inflicted on the people of the Virgin Islands, especially on the larger island of St. Croix. "Five years later, Hurricane Marilyn swept through St. Thomas uprooting everyone's lifestyles," said Marjorie in a voice filled with pain and sorrow. "Many other Caribbean islands were also badly affected. We can't tek another hurricane in these islands."

At the supermarket, people were scurrying about like ants gathering supplies in preparation for a long winter. Long lines were at the cashiers' counters extending way back into the congested aisles; people were becoming agitated and short-tempered. Packed and overflowing shopping carts were bumping against each other. The stores were running out of groceries; shelves were practically empty. Erma's mom barely was able to purchase some plastic plates, cups, flavored water, marshmallows, cookies, and Ritz crackers.

Upon their return to the house, Erma noticed that her mom was very tense and was continuously frowning. "Mother," she said. "I am a teenager now. I know about hurricanes. I see hurricanes on the Weather Channel, and I read stories about them. I learned about them in school!" Erma felt that her mother was protecting her, believing that she was too young to understand what was happening around them. "I am a big girl now," Erma muttered under her breath. "Mummy, you treat me like a child at times and at other times, you treat me like a woman. You don't ever treat me like a teenager. My friends' mothers do the same. Is it a Caribbean woman thing?"

"We live in the tropics, and hurricanes are a part of natural disasters that will affects us. I know about the dangers of natural disasters," said Erma boastfully. "I read that in 1867, three natural disasters affected the residents of the Virgin Islands." Marjorie's jaw dropped, and her mouth hung opened. "What do you know about them? I wasn't even born, much less you." Erma continued showing off her knowledge of Virgin Islands History. "I read about them in a history book from the public library at my school. There was a fire, a hurricane, an earthquake, and a tsunami all in one year!"

"You don't know Erma," her Mother sighed, releasing a long breath. "I dun live through two major hurricanes already! I don't want to go through any more hurricanes in my lifetime! I don't wish for you to experience any hurricanes. I won't wish one of dem on my worst enemy." Marjorie again began to recall the horrors of Hurricanes Hugo and Hurricane Marilyn - two major hurricanes that devastated the Caribbean Islands some years ago, the Virgin Islands included. Marjorie described in detail the damage and destruction brought about by the howling, furious winds and heavy rains. The high storm surge was terrifying. Roofs were blown off. Many people were displaced and had to relocate off island. "It was AWEFUL, Erma!" she tearfully concluded.

Now it all made sense to Erma. The thought of an imminent major hurricane was causing her mother to emotionally relive the experience of the previous storms. Marjorie hated the idea that Erma had to go through something similar. Erma began surfing the Internet and educating herself about Hurricanes Marilyn and Hugo, as well as on the approaching hurricane. She did not learn anything new that could erase the fear that was now creeping up her back. She plotted and tracked the coordinates for Hurricane Irma and realized that, indeed, Irma was heading directly towards the Virgin Islands; and as a result of its strength, serious destruction could occur. She now understood the worried looks on her mother's face, as well as the faces of other community members. As she continued her search, she learned about the *eye wall*, the *eye*, differences between storms and hurricanes, maximum sustained winds, and barometric pressure. Under different and normal circumstances, Erma would have enjoyed the knowledge gained about Mother Nature, but the information gained only brought on an anxiety that previously was not there. Now, she was in the same panic boat as her mother.

"Category 5?" Irma had been upgraded to a Category 5 hurricane. It was now Monday, and Irma was predicted to hit the Virgin Islands late Tuesday afternoon. Many took to the churches to pray for God's mercy and favor. A Category 5! Some people were even saying that Irma's winds were even stronger than a Category 5, but there were no more hurricane categories above 5. Erma could hear people talking about Hurricane Irma, as they passed outside her apartment building on their way down the road. Still, amidst all this, her friends continued to make fun of her. Erma just ignored them. "Maybe this school year, I'll have to get some new friends. These are too immature for me," she thought wisely.

The Governor of the Virgin Islands issued a curfew on the day the hurricane was due to arrive to the islands. He warned residents to take caution and heed all warnings. Radio announcers also began to plead with people to go to shelters, if they felt that their homes would be compromised during the hurricane. They were urged to do so before it was too late or too dangerous. It was unwise to venture out in the hurricane, after it had already started. Erma questioned her mother about going to a shelter. "Mommy," she pleaded, "can we leave now before it's too late?" Since this was the first hurricane that Erma would experience, she had no idea what to expect. However, based on what she had read and had been hearing, it was going to be a difficult time. Her mother, on the other hand, who can be a bit stubborn at times, adamantly replied, "No! I survived Marilyn and Hugo in this house, and I ain't going anywhere off of this property that my parents left for me."

Erma and her mother charged their phones and iPads. Neighbors came by to help board up the doors and windows of their house. Her mother fried some tasty chicken wings and Johnny cakes and packed them safely in plastic containers just in case the electricity went off. Erma kept looking towards her mother with a questioning expression. She strongly believed that it was "better to be safe than sorry" and prayed silently that her mother would take them to the shelter. The radio announcer continued to plead with the residents to go to the shelters early, before it became too dangerous to go outside. "Pack your bags and fill up your cars with gas. Leave now!" continuously begged the concerned radio announcer.

Reports began pouring in about the extensive destruction that hurricane Irma had already caused on other islands, as she continued her west northwest track towards the Virgin Islands. People were trying to make contact with friends and family who lived on different islands who already had come in contact with Irma, trying to find out about the fury. Marjorie tried contacting her younger sister who resided on the island of Dominica. She was unable to speak to her via her cell phone. She began to worry now for her sister and for her own safety. There were reports and videos from different media sources which spoke about the devastation left by Irma in Dominica, Anguilla, and St. Marten.

Erma's aunts and uncles on the U.S. mainland called and shared the stories they had heard and seen on social media. The island of Barbuda was completely devastated. Over ninety percent of the buildings and vehicles were destroyed, leaving one dead. St. Marten experienced seventy percent building destruction, with about twelve deaths, and many areas were flooded. Marjorie's family pleaded with her to evacuate,

"Irma is an out of control monster and very dangerous!" They told her to have a backup plan in the event that communication went down during the storm. An uncle living in Montserrat, who had experienced the trauma of the Soufriere Volcano, called and spoke to Marjorie; she placed the call on speaker phone and the words lingered in Erma's mind, "Marjorie, you went through Marilyn and Hugo; sure, but none of us have been through anything like this. Get out before it's too late!"

CHAPTER 4

Fear and Flight

Tuesday morning dawned and already there was a chill in the air. As Erma opened the door on the veranda to look outside she could feel the crisp, strong breeze blowing against her. She saw a few vehicles driving by. "They must be going to the shelter," she thought. All iPads, phones, and portable chargers were now fully charged. All houses on Erma's block were nailed and boarded up. Pets had been brought indoors and given plenty of water and food.

The full force of the hurricane was projected to arrive at about 2 p.m. At about 1 p.m, the power went out. Marjorie frantically burst into Erma's bedroom room and declared urgently, "Pack your bags! We have to leave now!" Erma hurried to her closet and came out with two garbage bags filled with items and her pillowcase. In the living room, her mother looked at her in amazement and asked, "When did you pack those? What are in those bags?" When Erma told her what was in the bags, Marjorie smiled and finally acknowledged that she truly had raised a smart and practical daughter. She accepted the fact that as a single mother she had done a fantastic job raising her daughter. "Thank you, Jesus," she whispered thankfully.

Marjorie realized that although she wanted to stay in her own home, it was not practical nor would it be a wise decision. Although the hurricane was miles away, its presence was already being felt, so it was "now or never" to leave their beloved home. The roof was already sighing under the pressure of the already strong winds. The wind was already sweeping the light rain under the doors, and the bathroom window was annoyingly banging. She really had to think about Erma's safety and not get choked up about watching over her mother's house. Now was the time to heed the warnings that were issued earlier. Marjorie looked at Erma and hoped that they still had time.

With teary eyes and heavy hearts, mother and daughter finally took their garbage bags and left the only place that they called "home." They both wondered if they would see their treasured home again. It was a struggle getting to the car because of the force of the wind. They had to lean forward with their heads bent down. They held tightly to each other and pressed forward. Marjorie drove as quickly as the wind pressure allowed her to drive towards the closest designated shelter which was not very far from where they were living. The rain was now falling a little heavier, and it was difficult to see ahead of them as the winds were smashing huge rain drops against the windscreen. It was a dangerous drive but, thankfully, Marjorie was a very skillful driver.

Finally, they arrived safely at the shelter. They were informed about the rules and guidelines of the shelter by a kind woman who was an American Red Cross volunteer. They were given a cot, a fluffy blanket, and a small bag containing toiletries like a toothbrush, toothpaste, and shampoos – each with the American Red Cross logo on it. They were treated to a meal. Then Erma and her mom, each lost in her own thoughts, laid down on a cot. Erma was on the cot thinking about her friends and wondering if they were safe. "Mom, do you think that my friends are safe? Do you think they are in another shelter?" she asked hopefully. But her mother's eyes were closed, and she was softly humming with King Obstinate from the island of Antigua as he sang, "How Great Thou Art" and "Wounded Soldier" on the local radio station WSTA. "Jesus," she prayed tearfully, "though wounded now, please do not let us die." The songs were soothing, filled with hope, and a promise of a brighter day from the Creator of the universe. The song and the announcer's voice made them feel safe throughout this terrible ordeal.

CHAPTER 5

A Night of Terror

The wind was howling eerily against the roof of the shelter. Lightning crackled, followed by the loud rolling noise of thunder. Occasionally, something would hit against the roof and bounce off. This somber litany went on for some time; it could have been for an hour, maybe two. It seemed like they were daring anyone to rise up and defy them. But Erma kept her eyes closed and tried to block out the hissing, and the howling, and the hurling happening outside. She was utterly terrified. All around her, there were strange noises; children were crying and screaming. Some adults were praying, and some were in the fetal position on their cots shaking, whimpering, and even screaming out every time they heard a loud thud on the roof. As Erma looked around her, fear and hopelessness was evident in the eyes of everyone present. Everyone was scared! Even the young men who did not seem concerned at first were now looking up in the roof of the shelter and then looking at each other in fear.

Suddenly, there was an ear-piercing sound. "Whoosh! Whoosh!" A gust of cold, wet air hit them, and then rain started pouring inside the shelter. The big room erupted into a bustle of confusion as people leapt from their cots grabbing bags and children, instantly causing cots and blankets to shift and spin around from the force of nature. All around, people were scrambling to grab something to hold on to, while others tried looking for their loved ones. No one was sure, as yet, of exactly what happened. Then, "BOOM! BOOM!" and "CRACK! SCREECH!" The roof of one end of the shelter suddenly peeled back, and in an instant was gone. Endless screams followed. It seemed to Erma like a scene from a horror film. A monster was terrorizing them. It appeared surreal, but it was happening; and it was happening to them now.

The shelter manager came to them and in a surprising calm voice told them that they had to relocate to another area of the shelter for a while. They hurriedly gathered their few belongings and willing followed the manager. She told them that as soon as there was a calm they would have to make a dash to the next shelter. Residents in the shelter formed a silent bond. They would unite and assist each other; they were all in it together. Men, who did not have any families, assisted single mothers and the elderly. The nurses in the shelter made certain that all pills were placed in secured bags, and everyone was waiting for the right moment to rush out.

A few hours later, one of the Red Cross volunteers shouted above all the noise, "Please listen up! It's unsafe to stay here! We have to evacuate to another shelter! It will be difficult, and at times even dangerous, but if you listen and follow the instructions given, we will make it! We will leave as soon as the eye passes!" Everyone quickly grabbed what bag was closest to them, parents hastily held on to their children, younger family members got the older folks together, and in a flash they were ready to follow instructions and make a quick dash through the door. "Keep your heads down and, if possible, place a bag over your head. Things may be flying around. Stay close to someone. When I say go, move! Carry as many people as you can in your vehicle. One! Two! Three! Go!" said the shelter manager in her calm voice.

With her bag of Johnny cakes and fried chicken in her hand, Erma held on to Marjorie with her other hand, and they both readied themselves for the dash to the car. Erma suspected that what Marjorie really wanted to do was to cuddle and comfort her. She tightly held on to her mother's hand and gave her a reassuring nod, indicating that she was alright. As they stepped out into the dark and raging night, Erma's hand was mistakenly and suddenly yanked from her mother's and she staggered back, slamming into the door post. "Mom!" she cried out. "Mom!" After a brief moment of silence, Marjorie's voice finally reached Erma in a croak, "I'm over here! I am ok. Don't worry. I'm ok."

At last they reached the vehicle wet, covered with tree leaves, and out of breath. A few other people filled into the back seats after them. Marjorie took a few seconds to catch her breath. Then without wasting any more time, she quickly started the car and drove along to the next shelter. Different objects peppered the vehicle, challenging its build and endurance, but the car kept pressing its way on the debris filled road.

The few miles drive seemed like an eternity away. Marjorie and Erma were engaged in prayer and crying out to God as the vehicle moved along. They finally managed, by some miracle, to arrive safely at the new shelter. The people there quickly ushered them inside, because they were expecting them. Once inside, all shoulders slumped in a collective sigh of relief. Some people even crumpled to the floor, crying and praying. A head count was then taken and all were accounted for and were safe. Together, they held hands and prayed giving thanks. Soon everyone was toweled dry and resting on new cots or blankets on the floor quietly praying and hoping that the rest of the night would go uneventful. (Well, as uneventful as a strong Category 5 storms passage can be.) With the eye having passed, the wind began blowing from a different direction. The monster continued to howl and rage, sometimes pounding on the door, on the roof or where ever it pleased. The howling winds were frightening and made many of the young people in the shelter cry.

CHAPTER 6

The Aftermath

Erma awoke to absolute quietness. She listened, but heard no sound. As her mind traveled back in time, she tried to gather her bearings; her eyes flew suddenly open, and she jolted to an upright position on the cot. Then, she felt the familiar hands of her mother gently touching her. Immediately all anxiety disappeared from her body, and she breathed a sigh of relief. "It's all over," she thought. "The hurricane has finally passed." Erma fell backwards, flat on her back, like a deflated doll. Was it a dream, or did she really just survived a night of terror - running and hiding from a monstrous hurricane that tried to steal more than just her name?

The residents looked outside and were amazed at what they saw. Tree branches were blown all over the place, and roof tops were scattered all over the streets. The nearby hospital was a disaster. Its roof had blown off. Poles were lying on the street, and windshields was blown out from cars in the parking lot of the shelter. The islands were now declared an emergency disaster area and under a curfew. The residents were not allowed to leave their homes or shelter until a specific time. It was reported that most of the roads were unsafe.

Residents began the process of clearing the debris and the poles, allowing cars and people to walk or drive by. Marjorie and Erma nervously left the shelter and drove home to see what had happened to their beloved home. They were worried about their house and the other houses around them; but to their joy and amazement, their house was still standing. More than half the roof, however, was blown away. As if on cue, tears began running down both of their faces when they saw that their house was still standing. What a beautiful house it was! It had weathered and withstood a Category 5 hurricane – another catastrophic hurricane! Many of their neighbors were not so lucky. Homes that were there before the storm were just a pile of rubble. Many roofs were lying on the ground in front of their houses, debris was piled up all around the streets, electrical poles were down, and wires were either lying around or hanging from trees. Fences had crumbled under the weight of fallen trees, and even vehicles were damaged by some of those fallen trees and limbs.

Erma was distraught. She did not know what to expect, but she was not expecting the horrific scene she saw in front of her eyes. Her neighborhood looked like a picture of a war zone. It was absolutely heartbreaking!

Since electrical poles were down everywhere, there was no power source. The cell phone communication towers were also damaged. There was no running water. Erma's aunt, Mabel, invited them to stay with her at her new house until their roof was repaired. Many residents gathered together and began the process of rebuilding. Residents began clearing their yards, as best as they could. Others got together to clear the streets so that vehicles could at least become much more mobile. The debris that was too big or heavy to move, they left for the workers with backhoes to remove. Days later, aid began to arrive from the United States of America, Puerto Rico, and other Caribbean Islands. Although down on their luck and not knowing how they were going to survive, residents of the ravaged US Virgin Islands were resilient and refused to buckle under the long and challenging days ahead.

Yes, challenging were the days ahead, but many people came together to help one another. Whether by way of cleaning up, sharing generators, offering storage space to neighbors who needed help, sharing food products, or even sharing the very clothes from personal wardrobes for those left with nothing, people assisted in the immediate aftermath. On the other hand, there were those who took a different path and worked against the spirit of togetherness. Individuals were waking up to discover their generators missing. Properties were being broken into, as if people had not suffered enough loss. A bad situation was being turned into a nightmare.

CHAPTER 7

An Unwanted Surprise.....12 days later!

Twelve days later, Hurricane Irma was walking from the neighborhood supermarket when she overheard a conversation about another Category 5 hurricane approaching the Caribbean Islands; and yet again, the Virgin Islands were in the projected path. Would Hurricane Irma experience another nightmare? Would Hurricane Irma have to race against Mother Nature once again? In shock and disbelief, Hurricane Irma hurried to her aunt's house to share what she had heard. As she burst into the house, and rushed into the living room, she was greeted by a radio announcer's voice, "and that is the latest update on Hurricane Maria who is making her way across the Caribbean, right on the heels of Hurricane Irma. We here at ..."

"So it is true!" Erma exclaimed in a half cry. This hurricane's name was Maria, and she was destined to follow the projected track of Irma. Were they not punished enough? Is Hell unleashing her fury on the people of the Virgin Islands? What was happening? This was unprecedented for any island to experience two major hurricanes back to back. Would this hurricane be in the Caribbean Sea or the Atlantic Ocean? Erma remembered that St. Croix was completely surrounded by the Caribbean Sea so if its projected path be located in that area, then the bigger island might surely be in its way. St. Thomas was already destroyed. Please, not another island in her lovely islands. She realized that her mother, who worked as a waitress in a hotel, would be gravely affected as St. Thomas and the Caribbean Islands were great tourist attractions.

Marjorie wailed hopelessly, "Not again, not another hurricane!" How can they…how can the islands withstand another major hurricane when they were still cleaning up after the last one? So many people were still living in shelters. Power, water, businesses…nothing was as yet normal! Residents were complaining that their homes could not withstand any more rain, much less another hurricane. People were on edge. All were astounded. But with a remnant of courage, they put their feet down and their heads together and began to make preparations for the onslaught of yet another Category 5 hurricane.

Residents tried to buy lumber to board up their homes and scrambled to purchase what food remained in the few stores which had found a way to open. This was no easy task, as many of these business providers had suffered damages from Erma. Lines at any store or shop were eternally long. Generators were now in great demand. Water, which was already scarce just before Irma, was a precious commodity, in any form, now. Everyone was in panic mode!

Mabel, Erma's aunt, had a higher paying job than Erma's mom. She had recently moved into her newly built house which was in a safer neighborhood. She invited the reluctant Marjorie to bring Erma and stay with her this time. They would need each other, but they could also support each other if the need arose. Marjorie felt reassured that they all would be safe and be together as a family this time, so she accepted the invitation. This huge house was located at the bottom of a steep hill, so Erma felt that the roof would most likely stay intact. The house was a three-story building, all the windows had built-in hurricane shutters, and the family felt just as hopeful as Marjorie sounded when she exclaimed, "Thank God! We will be safe here!" They did not think they would have to go to a shelter this second time around. They would be secure.

It was forecasted that Hurricane Maria would bring more rain than Hurricane Irma, so Erma felt that in the three-story house they would be safe. So as the hurricane approached, Erma wasn't as nervous as before. On that fateful day, she was relaxed and listening to her iPad. In fact, she was swaying to a song by Beyoncé: "Shining." Outside, the wind was picking up. The rain was pouring heavily, much more than with hurricane Irma. The thunder was roaring like an angry animal searching for its prey. Erma hated the sound of the wind, so she was glad she had in her ear plugs.

"BOOM!" The entire house suddenly shook. Erma jumped out of bed and ran quickly to her mom's room. "What was that?" They both looked at each other clueless and then ran towards Mabel's room. "What happened? What was that?" they demanded.

"I have no idea," replied Mabel, who rushed out of her bathroom with a face towel in hand. They walked the house from room to room trying to determine whether or not the loud noise had any connection to the house. They saw nothing, perhaps, mainly because all the hurricane shutters on the doors and windows were locked tightly. No sound immediately followed, so they decided to go back to their respective beds and lie down. Just shy of an hour later, Mabel and Marjorie entered Erma's room. Marjorie lightly shook Erma awake. "Come, Erma," she said in a frightened tone, "Come and see something." Erma quickly put her iPad aside from where it laid on her stomach and followed them. What Erma saw next was a scene she will never forget.

"What is that?" Erma asked, not really expecting anyone to answer. "Where is it coming from? How... how did it even get in?" The questions just kept tumbling out. How could this happen? This was supposed to be her safe haven. Everything was supposed to be perfect. Nothing was supposed to go wrong. What are they going to do now? Will they have to abandon the house and find a shelter? That would be an even more dangerous drive because of where Aunt Mabel lived. Plus, power had not yet returned, they were using a generator, and the roads were very dark. Mud was seeping through the second floor window. Where this mud was coming from no one could guess.

"What should we do?" Marjorie asked looking towards her sister. Mabel was lost in thought with a deep frown marring her features. Everyone just stared ahead at what was unfolding in front of them. Slowly, Aunt Mabel moved towards the window, studying it, moving from one side to the next. Then, in a flash, she started throwing out orders. "Erma, get the silver tape and scissors! Marjorie, you get some of the older bath towels, and I will get the mop bucket with water and anything else we might need! Hurry!" She yelled as she too moved to action. No one knew what was causing the thick muddy water to seep into the house, but it was clear that the shutter on the window had become unsecured, and now mud was oozing in through the corners, and underneath of a window on the second floor from the north where the bedrooms were located. The glass seemed to be leaning inward as if it was being pushed from the outside.

CHAPTER 8

Fight or Flight

All arrived almost at the same time back in the spot where the window was threating to cave in. A bigger mud puddle now covered the floor. The two sisters swiftly worked to clean up the window area with wet towels while Erma packed towels at the sides and based of the window. When the glass surface was rid of most of the mud, they quickly dried it, then plastered tape in crisped-crossed positions from top to bottom and left to right. Next, they removed the towels that Erma had secured in the space where the mud was previously piling in, replacing them with tapes to seal off the open space. Together, they attacked the mud on the floor. They shoveled and scraped it up as quickly as they could, dumping it into a trash pan. When they were finished, they stood with hands on hips, chests heaving, breathing deeply, and looking at the window. They had no idea how long the window would hold up with the tape, but at least it would slow down and reduce the volume of mud entering the house.

They prayed and asked God to protect them and the house and to allow the window to hold up and not collapse from any outside pressure. They agreed that they would all keep together in one bedroom. So, all three members of the family were now together in Mabel's room listening to the radio. In between listening, they discussed what they could do if the house suffered any major damaged. Abandoning the house in search of safety would be even more dangerous. Not only would they be exposing themselves to the elements of the hurricane, but the steep hill and all the surrounding trees and darkness could all result in a tragic outcome. They finally resolved that they would fight off as much as they could and pray that the hurricane would quickly pass before any massive destruction occurred. This time they were not going to run; they would grin and bear it. The dangers of running were greater than the dangers of staying in the house. What was frightening was that they did not know their neighbors or what houses surrounded them. It was their second time visiting Aunt Mabel just before the hurricane.

As they stored up their courage to remain in the house, the howling winds on the outside became louder, testing the family's new-found resolve to fight. The barrage of thunder was deafening, sounding as if it was directly over the house. The rain was pouring heavily from the skies onto the roof. The rain drops pelting against the house seemed like they would never stop. Erma peeped through the southern window and screamed, water was running like a river and overflowing the drain outside the window. Erma knew then that could not be an escape route. She wished that the rain would stop. It was raining cats and dogs outside.

At last the rain ended, the wind died down, and the thunder stopped. Erma knew then the eye of the hurricane had passed; she noticed the calm. Raindrops were no longer playing like the little drummer boy on the roof. Mabel seized this opportunity to open a shutter and look through the window. Her surprised gasp brought Marjorie and Erma rushing to her side. They pushed their heads against the window to see what could have caused Mabel to react like that.

Simultaneously, a similar gasp escaped them both. All the rocks and mud from the top of the hill had rolled down towards the house. Water was still rushing like a waterfall on the southern side. Marjorie went to open the door and, to her horror, found that it was jammed. They had nowhere to make an escape even if they were planning on do so. There was a window to the western side of the house but that was too high to climb down. The only way out of that window would be to use a ladder but that would be too risky. Where could they go, even if they wanted to go? What should they do?

The wind and rain started again, this time more furiously than before. Mabel, Marjorie, and Erma went back to check on the taped window where the mud was coming in earlier. To their disappointment, things appeared to be much worse than they were in the beginning. As they rounded the corner, they could see mud covering the floor from one end of the hall space and moving towards them on the other end. The bottom portion of the window was now broken and bucked inward, and the mud was piling in. Nothing could save the window now. They had no boards or means to board it up. There was no way they could stop what was happening and what was causing it to happen. They were certainly trapped now! Quickly, they dashed back to Mabel's room, locked the door and began to stuff towels at the base of the door to prevent any water or mud from seeping under. As the wind and rain began to pick up again, they all sat back on Mabel's bed glaring at the door and praying that the hurricane would soon be over.

The rain was again pouring heavily outside. Rocks were beginning to loudly bang against the outer door which was the only entrance to the second floor. "What should they do now?" they all wondered. Erma began to miss her father who had abandoned her and her mother to relocate to the mainland. This was a time when she wished that they had a strong male figure around to help make decisions and provide support. Could they stay put and overcome the horrors of nature's fury? How would they overcome these new challenges?

After several more hours of intense raging wind and rain pounding on the house, the winds finally subsided and the rain stopped beating against the roof. The ladies looked at each other wondering what their next move would be. Fortunately, no mud was able to escape into the bedroom past the towels they had stuffed at the bottom of the door. However, they had no idea what was waiting outside the door; no idea of what to expect. Timidly, they tip-toed towards the door. They stared, afraid and reluctant to open it, but they knew they had to. They didn't know how much longer they could remain locked in the room or if it was even safe to remain in the house at all.

Slowly, Mabel reached out and gripped the door knob firmly. With eyes bulging in fear, she looked at Marjorie and Erma. She took a deep breath, turned the door knob, and aggressively pulled on it. In a flash, and with a loud scream, all three ladies staggered backwards as the force of mud pushing against the door knocked them back into the room. Momentarily stunned, they stood there frozen. Then one of them yelled, "Shut the door!" They all leaped forward, and with joint efforts, began to push against the door with all their might until they successfully closed it. A few minutes later, they fell upon Mabel's bed exhausted, gasping for breath, and covered in mud.

Once their breathing stabilized, they began to plan their escape from the house as soon as the hurricane had completely stopped. They had to get out of the room, and they had to get out of the house. Not knowing what was happening outside of the house which was causing mud to pour into it was also a scary thing. They knew they could not get out through the entrance door because that was already stuck and blocked in. Marjorie mentioned a ladder that she had brought into the kitchen; it had been left behind by one of the men who helped her secure the house in preparation for the hurricane. The plan was to wade through the mud to get the ladder, and then use the ladder to climb down to the bottom floor from the window that Mabel had looked out hours earlier.

Wading through the mud took some time and much effort. The mud was about mid-calf high and the effort of trying to put one leg ahead of the other every time felt like they were walking with metal weights tied around their ankles. The mud, grudgingly, kept tugging on their clothes as if it wanted to tear them off. At last, they got the ladder and were standing before the window. Luckily, the mud had not reached the space on the other side of the house as yet; but there were mud and rocks below the window from which they were about to escape.

Mabel opened the widow and the light and fresh air that busted into the room was refreshing. They could now clearly see below and knew how to place the ladder. Marjorie lowered the ladder lightly, then they pushed hard on it forcing the ladder into the mud and rocks until it could not go anymore. Once she was certain that it would not shift, and was firmly grounded, she then brought the top of it a little below the window to lean against the house. They quickly and carefully climbed down the ladder: first Mabel, then Erma, followed by Marjorie.

Now they were all out of the house on the bottom floor. The mud was high to their knees making it difficult to maneuver a path through the rocks and mud stacked against the window. They were forced to leave their shoes in the soft, thick mud outside the window. Each of them, barefoot, suffered from cold feet which were hurting from having to step on rubble buried in the knee-deep, wet, mud.

Marjorie looked up the hill and her eyes opened wide in shock and amazement. "Oh, my God," she muttered sadly, "This is a new house. Why did this have to happen?" At the top of the hill, the top soil had eroded; it was where the soil and rocks that blocked the windows and door came from. Then Erma realized what it was that had fallen and shaken the house. The retaining wall outside of Mabel's house had been compromised from all of the rain and rocks hitting against it. The loud sound that they heard was the wall breaking and crumbling against the house. The pressure had caused the shutter to unhinge. Parts of the wall, with the rain water, were carried in the mud and came to rest against the shutters and the only door on that floor. And that is what was responsible for them being trapped in the house.

As they slowly moved around the house, they observed all the damage. The area where the vehicles were parked was so eroded that only the concrete road remained. The gut, on the southern side of the house, was angrily running over - still flowing like a river. Erma could not believe that a house this new had suffered this kind of damage. She felt like she wanted to faint. All the leaves and branches from the trees, that were not stripped bare by Irma twelve days earlier, were on the ground. Solar panels from her neighbor's roof were on the ground in front of the house. Roofs from other people's houses littered the hill. Debris was everywhere and in front of Mabel's house. Erma thought of taking pictures to remind her of the horrible ordeal, but then remembered that they left everything in their house when they escaped. The three ladies stood together looking up at the house in amazement, but sighed in relief. "Thank you Jesus. It is all over now," whispered Marjorie thankfully. "We are safe at last."

Erma left her iPad, her clothes that she treasured, her souvenirs, and even Mr. Chummy inside; but she was glad to be outside of the house. She couldn't believe what just happened. Marjorie, a very religious woman, began crying and praising God for once again sparing their lives. She realized that houses and materials things were not as important as she had previously thought. They could vanish in a moment, but faith and trust in God were more important than earthly possessions. They made their way up the hill and flagged down a rescue vehicle which took them back to the shelter, weary and battered.

CHAPTER 9

Acceptance

After some of the debris, once again, was cleared by the local and government agencies, the residents were able to visit and check on the welfare of other members of the community. It was an extremely emotional time – relief, joy, sadness, helplessness, and anxiety all mixed in one. People hugged each other, cried, and laughed; but most of all, people were just happy to see that they all survived another hurricane that they thought they would not have been able to endure. As she moved around St. Thomas, Erma was further astonished by damage and destruction that she saw.

Her church roof was completely blown away, many hotels were demolished or had suffered major damage, and her beloved school was a collection of rubble. Many other buildings were destroyed and had to be abandoned. Even the local University was severely damaged. The hospital was also extensively damaged on one side. Many patients had to travel on mercy flights to receive their medical treatment. The other two Virgin Islands suffered a similar fate, and it was clear that nothing escaped the wrath of these hurricanes.

"Irmaria," locally, was the term coined for the two hurricanes, Irma and Maria, which wreaked serious havoc not only in the Virgin Islands but throughout the Caribbean. One island that sustained very serious damage was the mountainous island of Dominica. The islands of St. Martin, Anguilla, and Tortola were also badly destroyed by these two very dangerous and powerful ladies. Puerto Rico, which is located to the west of St. Thomas, did not sustain much damage during the passing of Hurricane Irma but was not so lucky with Hurricane Maria. The residents of this neighboring island lent a helping hand to the people of St. Thomas after hurricane Irma, but Hurricane Maria literally left them crying out for the same benevolence that they had given so freely less than two weeks earlier. The other Caribbean islands, that did not sustain as much damage, provided much relief in terms of monetary donations and supplies. The Federal Government donated much needed supplies to the United States Virgin Islands. Residents stood in long lines, sometimes sitting in their folding chairs, waiting to obtain supplies of water, ice, and food.

Although Virgin Islanders had never experienced two major hurricanes back to back within days of each other, they have always been able to bounce back from hurricane destruction over the years. Just as they did after Hurricane Hugo and Marilyn, they did not sit back, complain, or blame anyone for their misfortune. Instead, they rolled up their sleeves, put on their charitable caps and work shoes, and began putting their islands back together. Friends and family allowed other family members, who were displaced, to live with them. Neighbors cooked for one another and even for strangers and visitors who were unable to leave the islands before the hurricanes struck. Many residents had to relocate to shelters, because their homes were unsafe to reside in. But with resiliency and strong determination, the residents of the ravished and once beautiful US Virgin islands began rebuilding their houses, schools, hospitals, supermarkets, and worked to restore all major service systems.

CHAPTER 10

School Finally Opened

A neighborhood radio station aired a report from the Virgin Islands Department of Education. Erma's school was scheduled to be opened. She was not as excited as she was earlier in August. She was still traumatized from her adventures with the two major Category 5 hurricanes. Her mother's story could not prepare her for the actual experience. Erma thought she had gotten it when her mother finally shared what she had been through. And in her mother's words, "It was AWEFUL! Oh what a race it was with nature!" Her value system had changed. She now realized that material possessions were not quite as important after all. Everything could be destroyed in the blink of an eye. What was important at this time was the value of human life; she promised to show her family, especially her mother, how much she loves and appreciates them.

The story of her Caribbean cruise dimmed in light of her most recent experiences. Where once the heckling she received from her friends bothered her, she vowed she would now smile. What's a little fun amongst friends, she thought? At least, they were all alive and well.

Some families, however were not as fortunate, and for them the devastation caused by these two hurricanes was overshadowed by five deaths that were directly related to the hurricanes. Three lives were taken during Irma on September 6th, and two during Maria on September 20th. One death in particular was deeply felt and commonly talked about was of a young Sergeant in the VI National Guard who died from blunt force trauma in his home when a portion of a neighbor's roof flew into his bedroom window. Another one as a result of Maria, caused Erma to shudder as she thought back on what she and her family went through. A victim in another area died due to blunt force trauma after being trapped in his house by a mudslide. His body was found four days later.

Communication was at an all-time low in the islands. Internet service was almost non-existent. There was no cable service on the island, and there was pretty much only one or two active radio stations; so young people were bored and restless. What could she do to occupy her time now? She found some books in a neighbor's house, and she began reading them. Her mother said it was a better past time activity, anyhow. The books turned out to be very exciting. She was now able to read the local newspaper more often, and she actually listened to the few radio stations which were still on air. She, however, missed the texting and other forms of social media. Erma remembered the curfews, so she stayed close to her home, unless she went to stand in lines to get supplies. She hated to stand in lines but felt she had to help her mother and aunt, especially with how dark it would be when night fell.

The First day of school came on the Tuesday after Puerto-Rico / Virgin Islands Friendship Day or as it's recognized on the mainland and nationally, Columbus Day. Upon arrival to school, Erma was surprised to find out that many of her friends had relocated to the Continental US. She was heartbroken. She felt that she didn't even get to say goodbye or exchange numbers with her friends. They didn't receive the much needed closure. She hoped in her heart that she would be able to reconnect with them one day.

The Department of Education offered counseling both individually and in groups to students to help them deal with their trauma. Though Erma was hurt and very angry, she said nothing. She truly missed her friends, especially Kezia. She knew they would have done the counseling together. It was one day that a counselor asked her to talk about her experiences that she finally opened up and spoke. She was very shaken up as she recalled her frightening encounters with Mother Nature. Erma began shaking and crying. She cried for a very long time, and finally, all the tension and emotions lifted. The fear, the anger...all were gone. Her heart was now free. At the end of the sessions, she finally began to heal mentally and was in turn able to help other friends. Erma spent summer 2017 building a story about her cruise through her escapades in the Caribbean, but now she has a different story to tell. Erma was glad that through the worst days of her life her family was with her. She now had hopes for a better tomorrow. This time, Erma's story is about the two times she raced against Mother Nature with all her wrath and fury!

THE END!!!!

ABOUT THE AUTHOR

Lorna Daniel resides on the beautiful Caribbean Island of St. Thomas in the United States Virgin Islands. Lorna received both her Bachelor of Arts in Psychology and her Masters of Arts in Guidance and School Counseling from the University of the Virgin Islands. Lorna has been an educator for over 35 years. She has taught all grade levels in the public school system. Lorna presently works at the Charlotte Amalie High School. She is an avid reader and hopes that young people everywhere will discover the joy of reading; and develop a thirst for knowledge. She hopes that in reading this book, others would realize that amidst the pain, loss and destruction experienced, with determination and resilience there is always hope for a brighter tomorrow.

www.ingramcontent.com/pod-product-compliance
Lightning Source LLC
Chambersburg PA
CBHW030546290526
45786CB00004B/1882